Poems to Count On

32 Terrific Poems and Activities to Help Teach Math Concepts

Sandra Liatsos

S C H O L A S T I C
PROFESSIONAL BOOKS

New York · Toronto · London · Auckland · Sydney

Cover design by Vincent Ceci and Frank Maiocco
Cover illustration by Stephanie Petersen
Interior design by Jaime Lucero and Roberto Dominguez/GrafiCo
Interior illustrations by John Jones and Kate Flanagan

ISBN 0-590-60340-X
Copyright © 1995 by Sandra O. Liatsos
All rights reserved.
Printed in the U.S.A.

12 11 10 9 8 7   8 9/9 0 1/0

Table of Contents

Math Poems

Shapes, Sorting and Patterning

Counting, Addition and Subtraction

Exploring Large Numbers

Measuring, Fractions and Graphing

Time and Money

Introduction

Why Pair Poetry With Math?

If we think of math as numbers and problems, it's hard to see where the poetry part fits in. But, if we broaden our idea of mathematics to include real-life experiences involving language, information, patterns, time, money, reasoning, thinking and playing, it makes sense that poetry should be a natural part of the whole. And if we remember how readily children are drawn to rhythm and rhyme, it's clear that math poems should be an important, powerful part of any math curriculum.

That's the thinking behind POEMS TO COUNT ON, a collection of 32 ready-to-use math poems and related activities. The poems are grouped according to the mathematical skills and concepts they explore. As you read through the poems you'll notice that sometimes the math is readily apparent, sometimes it's subtly woven into the poem's imagery. Either way, the activities that

accompany each poem will help you expand on the math possibilities present in each one. With practice, you'll begin to spot the mathematical possibilities in all of these and other poems that are already favorites of you and your students. Have fun helping your students discover the math in the poetry...and the poetry in the math.

General Suggestions for Using Math Poems

Begin by familiarizing yourself with the poems in this book. Then, you can try using math poems in lots of every day ways, such as:

• **to enhance your existing math curriculum.** Decide which poems would best support or round out what you're doing in math right now, then go ahead and share. Because they're already immersed in the math, children will be able to recognize the concepts when they bubble up in the poetry.

• to introduce a new math focus.
When you anticipate beginning a new math unit or focus, pull out a related math poem and begin with that first. After unearthing the math in the poem, explain to the children that you are going to be learning more about that topic in class. Then, from time to time, visit the poem again while introducing others throughout your study.

• as part of an interactive charts program.
Throughout the activities in this book you'll notice suggestions to turn some of the poems into charts. Actually, any one of the poems works perfectly as a chart. You can copy the poems onto a large piece of chart pad paper, or print the lines on individual sentence strips and display these on a pocket chart. You can have children match word cards or whole strips to place in the pocket chart. Or, children can write or draw word substitutions on removable sticky notes to place directly over words on chart pad charts. Be sure to look through the book for more chart suggestions.

• to create bulletin board displays.
Transfer a poem to a piece of chart pad paper or to a colorful piece of oak tag. Then, fix the poem to the middle of a bulletin board display. Surround the poem with the activities the children create in class and at home, or invite the class to provide an illustrated mural background to accompany the poem.

• to publish math/poetry portfolios. Make student copies of any poems you share in class and place these together with completed projects into a notebook or folder for children to treasure when completed.

• to begin a take-a-poem-home program.
To help strengthen the link between poetry and math, provide poems for children to take home and share on a regular basis. Support such an effort by asking children to complete a related activity at home. This book is chock-full of such take-home activities designed to build important home-school connections...and you're sure to dream up more of your own!

Bibliography

Books to Share with Children

Shapes, Sorting and Patterning

- *Look Around! A Book About Shapes* by Leonard Everett Fisher (Viking,1987). Observing shapes in everyday settings.
- *Ocean Parade* by Patricia MacCarthy (Dial, 1990). Offers opportunities for sorting activities and number problems.
- *Sea Shapes* by Suse MacDonald (Harcourt Brace Jovanovich, 1994). Discovering underwater shapes.

Counting, Addition and Subtraction

- *How Many Feet in the Bed* by Diane Johnston Hamm (Simon and Schuster, 1991). Helps children to learn to count by 2's.
- *Ten Black Dots* by Donald Crews (Greenwillow, 1986). Dot arrays inspire counting activities.
- *The Icky Bug Counting Book* by Jerry Pallotta (Charlesbridge, 1992). Children will delight in counting the bugs - and bug parts - featured in this book.
- *Twelve Ways to Get To Eleven* by Eve Merriam (Simon and Schuster, 1993). Fabulous book for exploring a variety of number combinations.

Exploring Large Numbers

- *How Much Is a Million?* by David Schwartz (Lothrop, Lee and Shepard, 1985). Introduces children to large number concepts.
- *Millions of Cats* by Wanda Gag (Scholastic, 1928). An oldie but goodie about how a husband and wife came to own a great number of cats.

Measurement and Estimation

- *Inch by Inch* by Leo Lionni (Astor Honor, 1960). Helps children explore the concept of an inch.
- *How Big Is a Foot?* by Rolf Myller (Antheneum, 1969). A classic tale about the importance of standard measurment.

Size, Fractions and Graphing

- *Eating Fractions* by Bruce McMillan (Scholastic, 1991). A picture book of foods cut into fractions.
- *I'm Too Small, You're Too Big* by Judy Barrett (Antheneum, 1981). Explores size comparisons.

Time and Money

- *Around the Clock* with Harriet By Betsy and Giulio Maestro (Crown, 1984). Learning about time.
- *Keeping Time* by Franklyn Branley (Houghton Mifflin, 1993). A nonfiction book about how we keep time.
- *The Story of Money* by Betsy Maestro (Clarion, 1993). A nonfiction book about money.

Resources for Parents and Teachers

- *Books You Can Count On: Linking Math and Literature* by Rachel Griffiths and Margaret Clyne (Heinemann,1988).
- *Exploring the Numbers 1 to 100:Activities, Learning Center Ideas and Celebrations* by Mary Beth Spann and the Teachers at Babylon Elementary School (Scholastic, 1993).
- *Literature-Based Math Activities* by Alison Abroms (Scholastic, 1992).
- *Read Any Good Math Lately?* David J. Whitin and Sandra Wilde (Heinemann,1992)

Math Poems

The Circle and the Square

"Let's run a race together,"
said the circle to the square.
"The curb will be the starting line;
that way it will be fair.
We'll roll as far as Farley Street
to reach the pizza place.
The loser buys a pizza
for the winner of the race."

"Easy words for you to say,"
complained the worried square.
"Easy enough for you to talk
about a race that's fair.
Because it's true that you can roll
to win a pizza race.
But I have pointed corners
so I can't roll any place."

"Don't worry," said the circle, then,
"I know what I can do.
I'll roll to Arthur's Auto Shop
and buy four wheels for you."

The circle rolled.
The square rolled, too.
They raced to the pizza place.
The pizzas jumped out of their pans
and cried, "We're in the race!"

They rolled up to the finish line
and cried, "Nobody's beat us!
So we can choose our prize, which is,
NO ONE'S ALLOWED TO EAT US!"

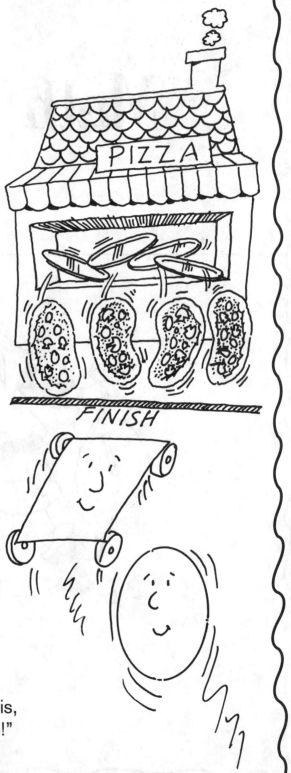

Before Sharing the Poem

Listening for Dilemma Details Before reading the poem to the group, tell children to listen for two problems that are described in the poem (i.e., the square can't roll and the pizzas refuse to be eaten). Ask children to then tell which of the dilemmas was solved in the poem (the circle bought wheels for the square) and which was not (the pizzas ran away). Have children offer ideas for how the second dilemma might be solved. (Tip: Children may need to listen to one or two careful read-throughs before they are able to identify the dilemmas.)

After Sharing the Poem

Shapely Pizzas Offer children prepared pizza shells (or individual English muffins) pizza sauce and cheese slices. Show children how they may use plastic knives or cookie cutters to cut the cheese into various geometric shapes (circles, squares, rectangles, triangles). Have children spread the sauce on the dough and then use the cheese shapes as decorative toppings. Challenge children to use the cheese to create patterns, pictures or faces on their pizzas. Have children take turns describe their geometrically-inspired culinary creations before heating, serving and snacking. (Tip: In addition to providing cheese as a topping, you may also offer children shapely steamed vegetables such as carrot coins or sliced fruits such as pineapple triangles (cut from rings) to use as toppings.)

Home-School Connection

Food Shape Collage Invite children to each take home a magazine featuring food advertisements and recipes. Have children comb through the magazine to discover and clip pictures of foods featuring geometric shapes (e.g., triangular wedges of cake, circular-shaped doughnuts, rectangular pieces of celery, etc.). Help children glue the food pictures on to a large piece of oak tag to create a food shape collage, or onto a series of mini-collages, each featuring food of a different geometric shape. Allow the edges of the pictures to overlap ever-so-slightly, so that students may use fine-line markers to outline the geometric shapes featured on the foods.

Triangle Riddle

I like to glide
        without a sound,
to pass a city,
        field, or town.
As pointed as a birthday hat,
        much larger than a tabby cat,
I stretch myself
        when breezes fly,
as if I'd like to ride the sky.
        On stormy days
                I'm taken down,
or else I tumble
        like a clown.
I ride the wind,
        I soar so high—
And now I ask you—
        What am I?

Before Sharing the Poem

About Mood and Imagery Tell the class that they are going to be listening to a riddle poem. Tell them also that to best solve the riddle, they will have to listen carefully to the moods and images (or mental pictures) the poem is trying to create. Suggest that children close their eyes and listen carefully as you read. When you are done reading, have children tell you whether or not they were able to see the poem's pictures in their minds. Also, have children try and guess the riddle. (Tip: If children had difficulty bringing images into focus, try reading the poem line-by-line so they have time to secure each image in their minds before moving on.)

After Sharing the Poem

Triangle Movement Cut several kite shapes from construction paper. Read the poem through and have groups of students pantomime the poem while each holding a paper kite. Comment specifically on how children use different moves to depict the same line. Also, try having children pantomime the poem without the use of the paper kites.

Home-School Connection

Triangle Treasures Have children each bring to school one triangular object (or an object decorated with triangles) and place these into a Mystery Triangle Box. Then, offer students a series of clues about each object and have children take turns guessing the identity of each one. Display the triangle treasures together with a label reading: Table-Top Triangle Museum.

What Creature Is This?

    We carve two triangles.
Each is an eye.
    We carve out one circle: a nose.
Then what will we carve underneath?
    A rectangular mouth,
with triangular teeth!
    But there are no elbows,
no shoulders, or toes.
    There isn't a body.
There isn't a brain.
    This head will not mind
if it sits in the rain,
    or if water pours out
of its mouth, eyes, and nose.
    What creature is this?
Is there someone who knows?
    (Hint: When Halloween comes
we'll make sure this head glows!)

Before Sharing the Poem

Listen Up! Tell children to listen carefully as you read the poem, because when you are finished, you will be asking them to answer the poem's riddle. When children have correctly identified the riddle answer as a "Jack O'Lantern," have them listen to the poem again and use crayons to draw the carved pumpkin as it's described.

After Sharing the Poem

Pumpkin Puss Provide each child with a large pumpkin shape cut from orange construction paper and an assortment of geometric shapes cut from black construction paper (circles, squares, triangles, ovals, rectangles, etc.). Have each child glue any number of black shapes onto the paper pumpkin to create a pumpkin face. Meet with each child to talk about the type and number of shapes they used. On the back of the pumpkin, glue a copy of the poem. Then, help the student record a pumpkin face word problem by counting and adding up the number of different shapes used, and then adding these numbers up to arrive at a sum of all shapes on the face.

Home-School Connection

Pumpkin Poetry Flannelboard Kit Use a highlighting marker to highlight the shape words on one copy of the poem: "triangles," "circle," and "rectangle." Mount on construction paper and laminate, if desired. Next, cut a large pumpkin shape from orange felt and an assortment of geometric shapes cut from black felt (circles, squares, triangles, ovals, rectangles, etc.). Finally, secure a small notebook and on the first page of the book write a note inviting families to share the poem and the kit, and then to jot their reactions and comments inside along with the date and their names. Place these items, along with a copy of the poem, into a large plastic food pouch with a self-sealing top. Have students take turns taking the pouch home, sharing the poem with their families and then using the pumpkin-shaped flannel board and geometric pieces to work out the poem. Show children how other shape words (and therefore other black flannelboard pieces) may be substituted for those highlighted in the copy of the poem. Encourage children to make up their own flannelboard pumpkin faces.

Cleaning Up My Room

My books and toys and clothes and shoes
    are jumbled in a heap.
I think I'd better sort them out.
    (That heap is getting deep!)
I'll pile the books with other books,
    the shoes with other shoes,
the clothes with clothes, the toys with toys.
    I'll put them where I choose,
all neatly placed inside my drawers,
    and in my closet, too.
My room will be so neat and clean
    that I will feel brand new.
And best of all when everything's
NOT in a mixed-up heap,
my bed will be so empty that
    I'll have a place to sleep!

Before Sharing the Poem

Clean-Up Tales Ask children to describe how their rooms look when at their messiest. Ask: Who cleans up your room when it is messy? Do you think cleaning up is harder than putting things away? Why? Does a messy room bother you or does it just bother other people in your family? Why?

After Sharing the Poem

Sorting Relay Offer teams of children a mixed-up box of toys and other objects collected from around the classroom. Have children attempt to sort and replace the objects to their rightful spots in the room before a timer buzzer sounds. Have children talk about how they decided to replace the objects in the places they chose. Ask them to think about how it would be to work and play in the classroom if every object was put away in a different, arbitrary spot each time it was used.

Home-School Connection

Toy Sort Invite children to each take home a magazine or catalog featuring pictures of toys. Have each child cut out ten toys. Back in class, have children work together to sort the toys into categories according to criteria of their choice (color, function, material [plastic, wooden, fabric], etc.). Then, have children glue the pictures onto oak tag or chart paper and use a marker to circle and label each group according to its criteria.

At the Laundry

"My goodness!" said the caterpillar.
"I am such a mixed-up messer!
I need help to sort these socks—
and put them neatly in my dresser.
Yellow socks, and orange socks,
purple socks, and green.
Red, and blue, and pink ones, too,
and striped ones in-between.
I've put them in the washer
and I've put them in the dryer.
And now they're in a jumbled heap
that keeps on growing higher."

"Don't worry," said the Katy-did,
"I'll help you sort them out—
the reds with reds, the blues with blues . . .
that's what it's all about.
We'll sort them all until
each color's standing in its pile.
With you and I both sorting,
we can do it with a smile."

"Oh, thank you," said the caterpillar.
"Come and have a seat.
Aren't you awfully glad that you
don't have so many feet?"

Before Sharing the Poem

This Is the Way We Wash Our Clothes Ask children to tell if they have ever helped with the laundry. Have them describe how doing the laundry at home differs from taking it to a self-service laundry. If possible, have the class take a walking trip to visit a self-service laundry. Maybe wash some articles from the classroom there.

After Sharing the Poem

Wash Day Math Ask children to tell all the steps involved in doing the laundry. Make a list of their responses and label each step with the math skill used to get the job done (sorting, matching, measuring, etc.). Children may be surprised to learn that such real-life math is a big part of laundry-day duties. Ask: what math skill is needed at a self-service laundry that is not needed when you do the wash at home? (Answer: counting money).

Home-School Connection

All Sorts O' Socks Have children each bring in one or two colorful pairs of socks from home. Ask children to place their socks into a laundry basket you place at the classroom doorway. When enough socks have been collected, separate the socks from their mates and mix well. Dump the sock collection on the floor and challenge teams of children to sort and match the socks up by placing matching socks together and folding over once. The team that sorts the fastest is the winner. (Tip: for a non-competitive version, have teams of students attempt to sort and match to beat their own best time.)

Animal Pattern Parade

I'm lining up my animals
to make a big parade,
a lion, then a chimpanzee
are marching in the shade.
A cheetah, then a chimpanzee
are marching right behind.
A hippo, then a chimpanzee
are following in line.
You may have guessed by now
the favorite animal for me.
In between two other beasts
I place a chimpanzee.

Before Sharing the Poem

Using Pattern Markers Read the poem through once to familiarize children with its sounds and rhythms. Then, read it through again, this time placing toy animals or counting markers on a table top to recreate the poem's animal pattern. Finally, try reading the poem while the children take turns placing the toys or markers.

After Sharing the Poem

Pattern Play Use toy animals, counting markers or game tokens, to build a variety of linear "parade" patterns for the children to identify and extend. If you are assigning an identity to an abstract game piece (i.e. if you wish for tokens to represent animals) expect children to only remember a few of these at one time. Remember that the markers or tokens themselves can be used to create any number of patterns. Children just beginning to recognize patterns will benefit from having you identify the pattern aloud as you point it out. Also, encourage children to build patterns for others to identify.

Home-School Connection

Patterns at Home Have children look at home for patterns that may exist there. Suggest they scout out patterns on items such as wallpaper, fabrics, food containers, toys, books, etc. Have children return to class prepared to describe their pattern finds in detail.

My Favorite Pajamas

A dog and a rabbit, a cow and two llamas,
  are walking all over my favorite pajamas.
A dog and a rabbit, a cow and two llamas
  are all on parade on my favorite pajamas.
They've lined up in order, and row upon row
  they stay in their places wherever they go.

All the dogs and the rabbits, the cows and the llamas
  are better to watch on my favorite pajamas,
Than shadows I see on my wall in the night.
  So, I think, for a while, I will keep on the light.

Before Sharing the Poem

Talking About Night Lights and Night Frights Ask the children to tell if they have ever been afraid of the dark. (Sometimes children are more eager to share such fears if they are asked to tell about a time in the past that they were fearful.) Have children tell how they coped with this fear. Record their answers on separate pieces of paper. Have students illustrate their responses and bind together into a class book titled, "Things to Do When You're Afraid of the Dark."

After Sharing the Poem

Shadow Patterns Using a film projector and a darkened classroom, have students create animal finger shadow patterns on the wall for others to guess. If students are unfamiliar with how to create finger shadow shapes, a hand shadow book such as *The Little Book Of Hand Shadows* by Phila H. Webb and Jane Corby (Running Press, 1990) will prove helpful.

Home-School Connection

Crazy-Mixed-Up Pattern Day Have children come to school dressed in wacky mismatched clothing combinations. Each piece of clothing must feature a distinct pattern and must not match anything else on that student. Tally the number of patterns represented by the whole class. Offer a prize for the student wearing the most patterned clothing pieces.

My Fruity Pattern

An apple and an orange, an apple and a plum, an apple and a nectarine,
Yummy, yummy, yum!
I've lined them up in a juicy row.
I'll eat from left to right,
A tasty apple every day,
Another fruit at night.

An apple and a grapefruit, an apple and a pear, an apple and an apricot,
I'll eat them anywhere.
I like to keep on adding
More fruit from left to right.
I'll add to my fruity pattern
Till it's out of sight!

Before Sharing the Poem

Collect Fake Fruit Ask children to use play clay to sculpt the fruit featured in the poem: six apples, an orange, a plum, a nectarine, a grapefruit, a pear and an apricot. Then, as you read the poem to the class, use these clay fruits to model the pattern described in the poem. You might follow this by showing samples of the real fruits. Have children arrange these from smallest to largest. Wrap a string around the each fruit; measure the string segment to discover that fruit's circumference.

After Sharing the Poem

Patterned Fruit Snacks Help students develop a list of simple pattern possibilities (A-B-A-B, AA-B-AA-B, AB-BA, etc.) Then, spread peanut butter, cream cheese or whipped topping on graham cracker rectangles. Invite students to use sliced fruits and berries to create such patterns on their crackers. Demonstrate how fruit types can substitute for the letters on your list. Have students take turns describing their fruity patterns for the class before eating.

Home-School Connection

Accordion Patterns Cut pieces of copy paper or drawing paper in half vertically. Staple two ends of the paper together to form a long strip of paper. Fold the papers accordion-style to create eight panels each. Have students take the papers home and use the panels to draw and label a simple A-B-A-B . . . picture pattern by illustrating objects of their choice.

Caterpillar Pete

"If I could multiply times two,"
said Caterpillar Pete,
"I'd figure out
how many shoes
I needed for my feet."
On winter mornings every foot
could snuggle in its slipper.
On summer mornings in the sea
each foot could flip a flipper."

"If I could multiply times two,"
the caterpillar cried,
"I'd know how many shoes to buy
by counting just one side!"

Before Sharing the Poem

Shoe Struggles Ask children to talk about the different types of footgear they own including shoes, socks, boots and other footwear (such as ice skates). Encourage them to be as specific as possible. For example, if they say they wear sneakers, ask them to tell what kind of sneakers. Jot each type of footwear onto an index card and then have the class work together to arrange the cards in a row ranging from "least difficult to get on " to "most difficult to get on." If children disagree about how the cards should be arranged, decide by a show of hands so that the majority opinion will be represented. Afterwards, try arranging the cards in a line on the bulletin board or wall. Attach a circular construction paper caterpillar head and tail to the line of cards to create a crawling caterpillar display.

After Sharing the Poem

Literature Connection Read *How Many Feet In The Bed?* by Diane Johnston Hamm (Simon and Schuster, 1991). Then, help children decide how many feet are in a small group of classmates, the entire class, the principal's office or the whole school. To help children begin learning how to skip-count by two's (or multiply by two), surround each pair of feet (belonging to a small group of students) with a circle of yarn. Then, count the total number of feet, whispering on the odd numbers and raising your voice on the even numbers, the multiples of two.

Home-School Connection

How Many Feet In Your Home? Have children trace and cut out feet shapes from construction paper. Mount pieces of lined paper onto the feet shapes and trim again. Divide each paper into two vertical columns labeled: Name / Number of Feet. Then, have the children take their paper feet home and conduct a family survey listing family members' names (including pets!) and the number of feet each member has. Back in class, help children each add up the number of feet featured on their surveys. Display the feet in order from least number of feet to most number of feet. (Tip: For a simplified version of this activity, just ask children to draw full-length views of family members and pets and then to draw circles around the pairs of feet. You can then help students arrive at a total by labeling the pairs with numbers counting by two.)

The Seesaw Ride

"Let's ride on the seesaw!"
the happy hippo cried.
"You monkeys take the other end.
We'll have a speedy ride."

The forty monkeys climbed on board,
although their end was high.
The hippo sat way down and waited
for his end to fly.

But the seesaw wouldn't budge.
"Oh, drat!" the hippo cried.
"If all you monkeys weighed a ton,
like me, we'd have a ride."

"Each one of us weighs forty pounds,"
they said, "not one ounce under!
How many of us would it take
to make you move, we wonder."

Another fifteen monkeys came,
and then one monkey more.
They jumped aboard and saw
the happy hippo start to soar.

Up and down they rode and rode,
The monkeys cried, "What fun!
We never knew that all together
we could weigh a ton!"

Before Sharing the Poem

Seesaw Stories Ask children to tell about their seesaw-riding experiences. Ask: How did you balance the two ends so that each rider had a chance to go up and down? If possible, visit a seesaw on a playground. Experiment with different numbers of children on each end to perfectly balance the board.

After Sharing the Poem

Cup Balance Explain that a seesaw is actually a lever that uses force at one end point to turn the lever around a second fixed point in order to lift a weight at the third point. Demonstrate this concept with a ruler balanced on a triangular-shaped block or pencil. Then, have children stack different numbers of pennies or dimes on one end of the ruler and then scout around the classroom to find small objects (blocks, erasers, counters, etc.) they think will balance the ruler seesaw. As you work, have students talk about how many objects they have to add or subtract from the scale to achieve a balance.

Home-School Connection

Balancing Act Show children a classroom balance scale and draw a comparison between the scale and a seesaw. After demonstrating the scale in class, ask children to bring in objects from home that they think will balance the scales. Try each set of objects out so students can see if they were right.

Ten,
    nine,
        eight,
they count with ease.
    Seven,
        six,
            five peas
left to go.
(Gorillas know peas make them grow.)
    Four,
        three,
            two peas,
now just one.

Gorillas gobble till they're done.

Peas

Before Sharing the Poem

Counting With Peas Before reading the poem, place ten dried peas or beans down on a table in front of the children. As you read, remove the number of peas as stated in the poem. Then, let the children take turns removing the peas as you read the poem for them.

After Sharing the Poem

Cup Math Show children any number of peas on a table. Count them together and then have the children hide their eyes while you use an inverted paper cup to conceal one or more of the peas. Children must then count the remaining peas and then guess how many peas are beneath the cup. Repeat the activity to develop a list of all the number combinations for each sum. Show children how the same three numbers may be expressed as an addition sentence or a subtraction sentence (e.g., $7-4 = 3$ or $4+3 = 7$). Use chart pad paper to record the number combinations you discover.

Home-School Connection

Pass the Peas, Please! Ask children to recount the various ways they manage to eat peas. Count the number of ways they come up with and compile their answers into a student-illustrated book featuring that number in the title, for example "25 Ways to Eat Peas."

A Guessing Game

Mrs. Festa put a feather
on her Sunday hat.
She added seven purple plums,
three fake birds
and a toy cat.
"How wonderful!" cried Mrs. Festa,
"I have room for more!"
She added two petunias,
and a plastic dinosaur,
three silver forks,
a wooden spoon,
a piece of frosted cake.
"Oh, what a fancy hat," she said,
"my new additions make."

But when she strutted out the door
the wind laughed right out loud.
"What a mixed-up hat," he huffed,
"to carry such a silly crowd."
He blew away the three fake birds,
the dinosaur, and cat.
How many things did the wind
leave on Mrs. Festa's hat?

Before Sharing the Poem

Hats Off! Tie a ribbon loosely around the crown of a large-brimmed hat and assemble the decorative items mentioned in the poem. (Tip: if you are missing any of the items, just cut replicas from felt or construction paper.) Invite one student to sit before the group wearing the hat. Distribute the rest of the items to children in the audience. As you read the poem, have students come up and insert the items in the hat band. Have other students act as the wind and remove hat items as indicatedby the poem.

After Sharing the Poem

Hat Alterations Using the hat and decorations described above, play a visual memory game. Have children hide their eyes while you add or subtract decorations to the hat. Children can then offer guesses about the alterations. Then, let the children take turns adding and subtracting items for other classmates to guess.

Home-School Connection

Crazy Hat Day Have children decorate hats and caps at home to wear to school on "Crazy Hat Day." Encourage children to embellish their hats with silly or outrageous decorations. Count the number of zany decorations each child attaches to his or her hat. Then, tally the total number of decorations represented by the class.

Ten Little Pups

Ten little pups
walking in a line.
One chased a butterfly.
Then there were nine.

Nine little pups
running through a gate.
One ducked behind a post.
Then there were eight.

Eight little pups
see a boy named Kevin.
One followed after him.
Then there were seven.

Seven little pups
doing puppy tricks.
One jumped behind a rock.
Then there were six.

Six little pups
playing by a hive.
One found a hollow log.
Then there were five.

Five little pups
wanting to explore.
One wandered down a stream.
Then there were four.

Four little pups
running round a tree.
One flopped and fell asleep.
Then there were three.

Three little pups
playing peekaboo.
One hid behind a bush.
Then there were two.

Two little pups
fighting just for fun.
One growled and ran away.
Then there was one.

One little pup,
looking for a brother,
found every one of them
and brought them to his mother.

Before Sharing the Poem

Finger Pup-ets Use fabric paints or markers to decorate each of the ten fingers of a pair of gardening gloves to resemble dogs' faces (or ask children to do this for you). Then, wear the gloves and display the finger pups as you read the poem. Fold fingers down as dogs are described leaving. Invite children to take turns wearing the gloves as you recite the poem.

After Sharing the Poem

Puppy Act Ask ten children to act the parts of the pups in the poem. Pin dog tags numbered 1–10 on the pups so they will know which dog is the next to leave. (Pup #10 should leave first; pup #1 should leave last.) The children should listen carefully as the poem is read so they can act out what is happening as well as leave when the poem says to do so.

Home-School Connection

Collections of Ten Invite children to bring collections of ten toys each. (the toys should be ten of the same type toy, such as ten dinosaurs, ten cars, ten teddy bears, etc.) Then, use the toys to enact the poem. As you read, modify the poem by changing the word "pup" to a word labeling the toys the children provide.

The Dog Hotel

Five poodles came
to spend the night.
They sat to watch T.V.

Five dachshunds came
to spend the night.
They ate hotdogs with me.

Five German shepherds
spent the night.
They jumped on all the chairs.

Five Yorkshire terriers
spent the night.
They ran up all the stairs.

"Bedtime!" I called.
"Let's stop before
another bunch arrives.

To see how many
beds you need,
I'll count you all by fives!"

Before Sharing the Poem

Pets are People, Too! Ask how many children in the class own a dog. Have them tell what their dogs like to do to have fun. Ask the children to tell about other pets they own and what they like to do to have fun. Can they tell when their pets feel sad, afraid or angry? How?

After Sharing the Poem

Five Alive Ask children to estimate how many fingers there are in the classroom. Then, count the actual amount by fives. Check your work on a hundreds' chart by using markers or chips to cover over the multiples of five. Ask: Can you see a pattern if we cover over every fifth number on the chart? Then, have children estimate how many toes are in the class. Count these by five, too. Follow up by having students do a tempera paint hand and foot print collage on a mural paper. When dry, number the fingers and toes to arrive at a grand total number of digits.

Home-School Connection

Toy Collections Have children bring in toy collections, each containing five items. Some possibilities might include five toy trucks, five dolls, five toy dinosaures, five Display these together on a table. Count by five to see how many toys are on display altogether.

Bird Math

I'm counting all the sparrows
that are landing in our yard,
and all the squawking blue jays.
Adding really isn't hard.

But now the sparrows fly away.
There go two—and four.
I must subtract them
from nine jays.
But here come fourteen more!
So I guess I'll add again,
or should I multiply???

Math starts getting
harder when
the birds decide to fly!

Before Sharing the Poem

Bird Talk Ask children to tell if, where and when they have ever watched birds feed outside. Have them tell what happens when they try to count the number of birds they see. Ask: What causes the birds to fly? After the children have had a chance to talk, tell them they are going to listen to a poem about a birdwatcher who is having trouble counting the birds in her yard.

After Sharing the Poem

Study One Square Share the book *One Small Square* by Donald Silver (W.H. Freeman and Co., 1993). Divide children into pairs or small groups. Take children out for a nature walk and focus each pair or group on a small piece of land. Use yarn or string to stake out the areas under investigation. Have children note and count the number of plants or animals that come and go or grow on the area.

Home-School Connection

Bird Watch Encourage students to bird-watch on their way home from school, or at home. Show children bird identification guides and have them notice the number of different species they can identify. In class, have students keep a running list of bird species they have identified. Next to each species, have students place illustrations plus tally marks noting the number of times that bird type has been cited.

One Hundred Cats

A hatmaker living in Klats
ended up with one hundred young cats.
Though she started with ten,
all the others came when
they saw the ten wearing new hats.

Before Sharing the Poem

Rebus Cat Chart Copy the poem onto a large piece of chart pad paper, leaving plenty of space between lines. After reading the poem to the class, suggest that the children draw small illustrations above any words that can be illustrated, thus turning the chart into a rebus poem. Read the poem together again. Another time, try using self-sticking notes to cover up the words, and have the children "read the pictures" as they come up in the poem.

After Sharing the Poem

100's Cats in Hats Divide the number 100 by the number of children in your class. Give each student that number of 3-inch square removable self-sticking notes (all the same color). Tell students to use each of the notes to draw a little picture of a cat in a hat. Collect the completed notes and stick them to a piece of oak tag or to a bulletin board to create a 10 inch x10 inch array of cat pictures. Count the pictures together to determine that there are indeed 100. Number the pictures, if desired. Ask: How many groups of ten cats are in this picture?

Home-School Connection

Thumb Print Kitties Offer students a take-home print kit containing a washable ink pad, a set of fineline markers, paper. Include directions telling students to use the supplies to make 100 of their thumbprints into 100 cats. Bind the pages into a class book titled with the number of thumbprint cats inside (i.e., "Our Book of 2500 Thumbprint Cats!").

A Speedy Young Driver

A speedy young driver from Gar
always added more wheels to his car.
    "I once thought ten or twenty,"
    he said, "were just plenty,
but a hundred are better by far."

That daring young driver from Gar
added eighty more wheels to his car.
    With a hundred in place
    those wheels ran out of space,
so he added more floor to his car.

Before Sharing the Poem

Assembly Line Drawing Assemble a small group of children around a table. Read the poem through and tell children that they are going to use an assembly line method of drawing to "assemble" a picture of the car. Ask if anyone knows how an assembly line works. Tell children that automobiles are most often built this way, with people or machines adding parts as the car being built moves down the line. Then, use a large piece of drawing paper to draw a racing auto body. Pass the paper to the child next to you and ask that child to add up to ten wheels to the car before passing the car on to the next student, who may add up to ten more wheels. Continue passing the paper car around (while counting outloud, if desired) until the car has 100 wheels.

After Sharing the Poem

100 Wheelies Chart Ask children to bring in bottle caps. Save these until you have 100 caps in all. Then, arrange and glue these to a chart as suggested in the illustration. Have students draw trucks and cars around each set of wheels. Number the wheels in the space below each one, if desired.

Home-School Connection

Wheel-Life Estimation Have children take time to estimate the number of wheels they have at home. Record their guesses on a piece of chart pad paper. Then, offer each student a "Wheel Check List" listing possible wheel locations students may have mentally overlooked (on vehicles, on strollers and carriages, on toys, on carts, in drawers, on luggage, beneath furniture, etc.). Have students take the checklists home and return to school with tally counts noting the wheels they counted. Compare these figures with the original estimations to see who came the closest.

At Bedtime

Mom and Dad just told me,
"Son, if ever you can't sleep,
it's best to close your tired eyes
and count one hundred sheep."
I'll take my Mom's and Dad's advice,
And count them on the wall.
Eleven sheep are running by.
I wish they'd hear me call.

Now twenty sheep, and thirteen more
are leaping on the ceiling.
My room is really jumping now,
and jumpy's how I'm feeling.
Now forty sheep are rolling
on my floor, and sixteen more
are sleeping underneath my bed.
(I wish they wouldn't snore.)

I think my Mom and Dad were wrong -
I'll never sleep this way . . .
Instead I'll count one hundred
chimpanzees who want to play.

Before Sharing the Poem

Pillow Talk Talk with the class to discover what the children do when they can't get to sleep. List their answers on a piece of chart pad paper. Ask if any of them ever hear of counting sheep to get sleepy.

After Sharing the Poem

100 Sleepy Sheep Glue 100 cotton ball, to a piece of oak tag. Use glued-on bits of black felt and fineline markers to add details that will turn the balls into sheep. Label the chart : "Can you count these sheep without falling asleep?"

Home-School Connection

Sleepy Sheep Bedtime Companion Place a small stuffed sheep or lamb puppet, a few bedtime storybooks and a journal notebook into a backpack. Let children take turns carting the backpack home with them so the sheep can visit overnight. In the front of the journal, jot directions to parents asking that they help their children log journal entries about the visit. Back in class, have the caretaker child volunteer to share his or her journal entry aloud.

Peter Anthony

"I have a million alligators
swimming in my pool,"
says Peter Anthony
Paul Meredith O'Toole.
"I have a thousand buffalo
out grazing in my yard,"
says Peter Anthony, "I ride them
'cause it isn't hard.
A zillion zebras on my bed
are jumping right this minute,"
he says, "and I will join their game
because I know I'll win it."
He hurries off
and leaves me thinking
while I bounce my ball,
"Poor Peter Anthony—that kid
just cannot count at all."

Before Sharing the Poem

Tall Tales Ask children to tell if they know what is meant by "exaggeration." When they understand the meaning of the word, ask them to tell about people they know who exaggerate (no names, please!). Then, tell them they are going to listen to a poem about just such a person. Tell them to listen for the exaggerated claims in the poem.

After Sharing the Poem

Big Name Numbers Print the poem on the chalkboard or copy onto a large piece of chart pad paper. Ask children to identify the words that represent large numbers. Ask if they know of any other large number words and add these to the space beneath the poem. Talk about times these words might come in handy.

Home-School Connection

Play "Can You Top This?" This is a perfect dinner table game to send home with students. (You might want to practice in class before having children teach their families how to play.) Begin by having player #1 tell a tall tale sentence involving the number one (i.e., "I found one dollar today."). Then, player #2 tells an even taller tale incorporating what player #1 has said, plus the number two (i.e., "I can top that; I found one dollar dancing on two pigs.") Player #3 then follows suit (i.e., "I can top that; I found one dollar dancing on two pigs who were eating three ears of corn."). Play continues around the table as long as enthusiasm and memory stays strong.

The Tickbird to the Flea

"It really doesn't matter,"
said the tickbird to the flea,
"that there are taller creatures
who can tower over me.

The lion may be bigger,
but he doesn't have a beak.
The hippo may be wider,
but he can't play hide-and-seek.

The monkey is enormous
when he's swinging from a tree,
but he throws bananas at his friends:
Would you do that to me?

Oh, I'm happy that I'm shorter.
Yes, I'm lucky that I'm me.
In fact, I'm quite gigantic
standing next to you, dear flea."

Before Sharing the Poem

A Bird's Eye View Ask the children to tell how important size is to them in their lives. (For some children, size is a big deal; for others it's not very consequential.) Tell the class you are going to read a poem about a tickbird who feels small compared to other animals and who is trying to feel big by comparing its size to a flea's. (Tip: If the children are not familiar with tickbirds, locate a picture of one in an illustrated bird guide and share the bird's statistics with the class.)

After Sharing the Poem

Sizing 'Em Up As children may be sensitive about height, ask several parents or colleagues to help you out with this activity. Select two people to stand next to each other. Have the children tell who is taller. Then, have children continue to arrange more people in the line from shortest to tallest. Have them rearrange the line so that the tallest person is in the middle and the shortest people are on the two ends. (This will require children to find people of almost-matching heights to "bookend" each other as the height line descends).

Home-School Connection

Relative Size In class, have children make a list of their relatives from tallest to shortest. Have them guess the height of each person on their lists (in feet and inches). Then, have students take their lists home to check them against the real thing. Have children record the actual heights of the relatives next to their guesses. Did students have any surprises?

The Inchworm's Trip

Inch,
   by inch,
      by inch
         he crawls

through our classrooms,
   through our halls.
He's one inch long
   and will not stop,
Inching, inching,
   past the mop.
Inching, inching,
   up my chair.
Now he's inching
   through my hair—
His way of "walking's"
   fun to see—
Does it tickle him
   as much as me?

Before Sharing the Poem

Exploring The Inch Ask children to tell what they know about an inch: how big it is, what it is used for. Show children an inch on a ruler. Then, use a tape measure to measure the height of each one of them, in inches! Ask, too, if any of them has ever seen an inch worm and if they can guess how the inch worm got its name. Have children tell if they think the inch worm is exactly an inch long. Then have them research to find out if they were correct.

After Sharing the Poem

Ticklish Riddle Talk with children about the double meaning of the word tickle in the last stanza of the poem: "Does it tickle him as much as me?" If children are stumped, tell them that the word "tickle" has two meanings: to physically "tickle" as the worm does to the child's skin—and to delight, as the inch worm's "inching" does to the child when she sees it. Ask: Which meaning is being referred to in the last line of the poem?

Home-School Connection

Inch Hunt Offer students each a ruler to take home and use to locate inch-long or inch-wide things at home. Have students first measure and then record their inchy items on lengths of adding machine tape. Provide time in class for children to share their lists. Then, tape all the lists together, add an inch worm head and tail cut from construction paper. Provide the inchworm with a dialogue balloon that says, "Read our big list of inchy items!"

The Old Man from Hampstead

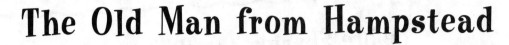

A tired old man from Hampstead
could never sleep well in his bed.
"If I'd learned how to measure,"
he said, "what a pleasure.
I'd have enough room for my head."

Before Sharing the Poem

Linking Math and Limericks Tell the children that they are going to hear a limerick: a five-line poem set in a particular rhythm. Ask the children to see if they can listen for the math problem in this poem. After reading the poem, ask the children if the poem's rhythm sounded familiar. Then share other favorite limericks and count the lines in those, too.

After Sharing the Poem

Master List of Measuring Have students brainstorm a list of things we can measure at home as well as a separate list of measuring tools used to do the jobs. To aid your efforts, have students envision one room or area of the house at a time. On a large piece of chart pad paper jot a list of things that might need measuring in each area. Don't forget to include the basement, the laundry room, the attic and the garage, etc. Have students return home to scout for items they may have forgotten about. Add these to your list before posting it in the classroom.

Home-School Connection

Foot-Long Measurers Invite children to take tape measures and rulers home to measure the shoes in their houses. Have them find out who wears the longest shoes, the shortest shoes, the widest shoes and the highest-heeled shoes. Children may wish to graph their results.

First Prize in
the Bean Contest

Guess how many jumping beans
  Are jumping in the jar.
Guess how many jumping beans
  And you will travel far.
Guess the sum of jumping beans
  And you'll be first to go
Jumping

        .   .   a   .
like ·   ·   ·   ·   . jumping
                        ·   ·   . bean

From here to Pocono.

Before Sharing the Poem

Counting Beans Ask the children if they have ever heard of a bean jar guessing contest. Bring a large mayonnaise jar filled with dried beans to class. Have students estimate how many beans are in the jar. Have them describe how they decided on their guesses. Then, provide copies of hundred's charts for children to use as counting mats so they can count them without error.

After Sharing the Poem

Bean Jar Guess Collect enough baby food jars so that each student has one. Fill the jars with jelly beans—keep a list of how many beans you place in each one. Stick a masking tape label to each jar and print the sudent's name on the label. Provide students with a supply of removable mini self-sticking notes. Have each student guess how many beans are in his or her jar by jotting a guess on a sticky note and sticking the note onto the jar. At day's end you can check the guesses against your list. Ask students who came up with approximate estimates to share their strategies. You might want to write the strategies and display for all to see. Allow students to take their jelly bean jars home to enjoy!

Home-School Connection

Jumping Bean Contest Have children practice jumping on one or both feet at home. Then, in class, hold a jump-a-thon to see who can jump the most in a minute or who can jump the longest without needing a rest. Tally up the number of individual jumps as well as the total number of jumps performed by the whole class.

The Robins and the Worm(s)

Two robins had a tug of war
to win a skinny worm.
Each pulled and tugged
and stretched an end.
The poor worm tried to squirm.

At last the robins dropped the worm.
"Cut it in half," said one.
"Half for me and half for you."
He chopped and it was done.

But then the robins had a fight
about which half was whose.
No matter how they squawked
and squabbled
neither bird would choose.

The worm halves quickly crawled away.
Each found a secret hole,
And there it grew and grew until
each half became a whole.

Before Sharing the Poem

Sharing the Spoils Have children talk about the difficulties of sharing with friends and siblings. Ask: Is it easier to be a child who must share, or the child who wants someone to share with them? Why is it so hard to share? Why does the dividing up so often seem unfair?

After Sharing the Poem

Halves vs. Parts Ask children to tell what is wrong with the following statement: "He got the bigger half!" Explain to children that the first half of something always is exactly the same size as the second half. If a whole is divided into two unequal parts then you have two parts or pieces, but you don't have halves. Demonstrate this idea by cutting some soft cookies into two equal halves and others into two unequal pieces. Then eat your demonstration.

Home-School Connection

Cut-In-Half Snack Party Have children bring a healthful snack to school that has already been cut in half. Then, have children keep one half of their snacks and place the other half on a number on the snack table. Have children reach in a box or bag and pull numbers that correspond to those on the table. They may then go to the table to locate the halved snack that matches their number. (Tip: To help students avoid confusion, ask families to send in snacks that must be cut in half, not counted and divided in half.)

Dividing the Pie

"Now is the time
for dividing the pie,"
the grasshopper said
to the blue-bottle fly.
"Don't forget us!"
cried the ant and the cricket.
"Nor me," said the spider.
"Do I need a ticket?"
"No, no," said the grasshopper
holding his knife,
"We'll each have a piece
and give one to my wife.
But, first, can you tell me
a way to divide
a pie that is frozen
completely inside?"

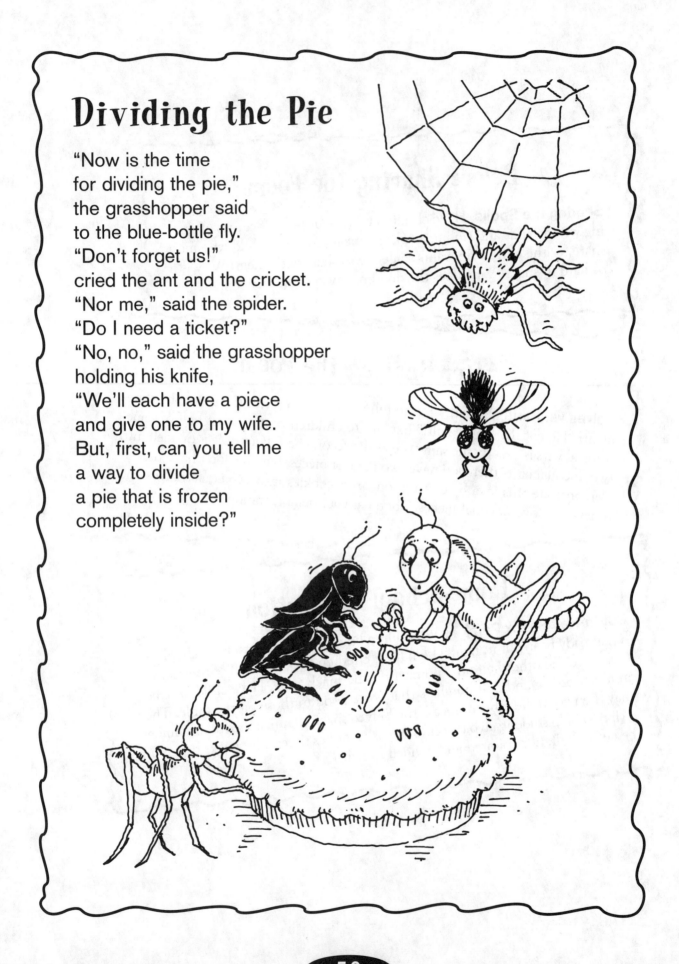

Before Sharing the Poem

Listen Up! Have children get ready to listen for the problem posed in the poem. After reading the poem ask: How would you suggest solving the problem? Has your family ever run into difficulty when preparing or dividing up food?

After Sharing the Poem

Divide and Conquer Offer children copies of the poem and have them tell how many pieces of pie the grasshopper must serve (6). Draw a circle on the back of each paper and have children use pencil lines to show how the grasshopper may cut the pie into six equal pieces. Talk about how each of these pieces represents a fractional amount (1/6) of the whole.

Home-School Connection

Interview the Cook Ask children to interview the grown-up who prepares most of the meals in the house to discover how he or she knows how much food to make so there is enough for everyone who is eating. Have them ask the cook to tell if they ever made any measurement mistakes. Finally, ask the cook to contribute a favorite recipe featuring fractions plus a measurement tip which may be bound into a class cook book.

The Giraffe Graph

"My son," said the mother giraffe,
"very soon you'll grow bigger by half.
   Each month we will measure
   your height. What a pleasure
to show each new inch on a graph."

"I'll draw myself," said the giraffe
"growing taller each month on my graph.
   I'll soon be so tall
   I'll go right off the wall,
and that will make both of us laugh."

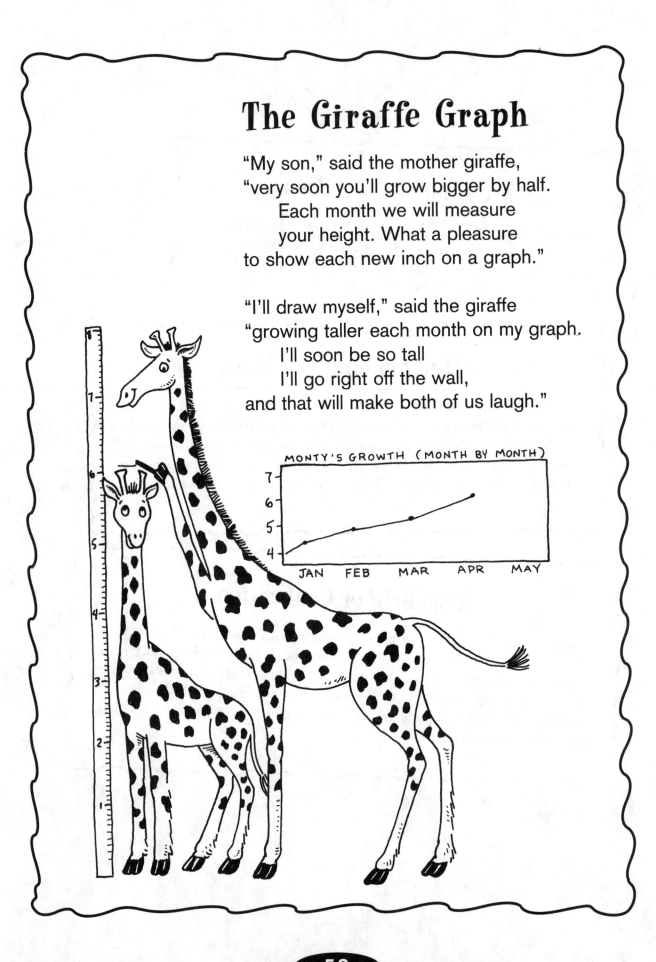

MONTY'S GROWTH (MONTH BY MONTH)

JAN   FEB   MAR   APR   MAY

Before Sharing the Poem

So Big! Ask the children to tell if their families keep ongoing records of their growth (wallmarks to indicate height, medical records, scrapbooks filled with memories, photo albums crammed with pictures taken through the years, etc.). Ask children to tell why grown-ups might keep such growth markers. Then, tell children they are going to hear a little poem about a mother giraffe who is trying to keep track of her child's growth spurts.

After Sharing the Poem

Height Awareness Ask children to tell if they each know their height in inches. Record their guesses and then use a wall height chart to get an accurate height reading of each child. Repeat the activity by estimating and then measuring (with a tape measure) other body parts: ears, wrists, shin bones, thumbs, smiles, etc.

Home-School Connection

How Long Was I? Have students find out from their families how long and how heavy they were at birth. Have students return to school with these statistics and then plot them on two separate line graphs as shown in the picture. Is the longest (or shortest) child at birth now the tallest (or shortest) one in class?

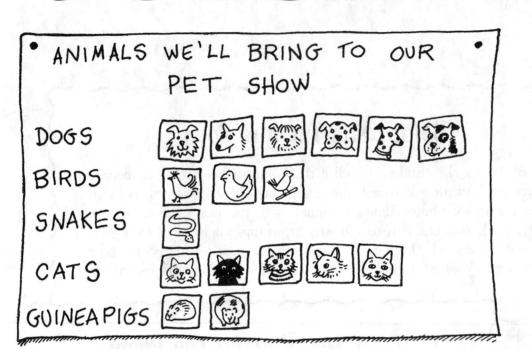

ANIMALS WE'LL BRING TO OUR PET SHOW

DOGS
BIRDS
SNAKES
CATS
GUINEA PIGS

The Pet Graph

Our pets are dogs, and mice, and birds,
and rabbits, fish and cats,
and other pets, like guinea pigs,
and gerbils, snakes, and rats.
We'll put their pictures on a graph;
the dogs will have their row.
The snakes and cats will each have theirs,
Each other kind also.
We'll hang the pet graph on the wall.
Each row of pets will show
how many of each kind our class
will bring to the pet show.
We hope to see a parrot or
a monkey on the graph.
And if we see them in the show
we know they'll make us laugh.

Before Sharing the Poem

Pet Survey Ask children to raise their hands if they have 100 pets. Then ask them to raise their hands if they have ten pets (then nine pets, eight pets, seven pets and so on, down to no pets). Ask children to tell why (almost) no one had 100 pets, while many children had one or two pets. Then tell children they are going to hear a poem about a class that tried to count the number of pets they owned.

After Sharing the Poem

Graphing Pets Offer children index cards so they can draw pictures of the pets they have at home. Instruct children to use one card for each different type of animal. For example, if a child has a French poodle and an aquarium full of fish, have her draw a few fish on one card and the dog on another. In the corner of each card, the children may print the number of that kind of animal they own. On a bulletin board display, use the cards to make a bar graph showing each kind of pet. Help children count the number of pets in each category (by adding up the numbers of index cards displayed) as well as the total number of animals owned (by adding up the numbers in the corners of the cards).

Home-School Connection

Pet Visitors Send a note home inviting parents to bring family pets in to class for a visit. Ask parents to sign-up for specific visitation times. (Tip: First thing in the morning works well because then the animal can visit while the parent is there, and then, if the animal is not a small bird, reptile or rodent, the parent can take the animal back home after the visit is over.) Be sure to have students prepare a list of questions in anticipation of the pet's visit, and suggest that students follow-up with a thank you note to the parent who took the time to come in with the pet.

The Birthday Graph

"I have so many children,"
the mother rabbit said,
"I cannot keep
their birthdays straight,
at all, inside my head.
There are birthdays every month
but I forget how many,
and whose is when,
or if the Birthday Bunny's
Bill, or Benny,
or Oliver, or Angela,
or Lionel, or Paul -
it's really quite a problem,
'cause, you see,
I love them all!
But if I mark their birthdays,
on a graph
across my wall,
then every month I'll surely see
the birthdays of them all."

Before Sharing the Poem

Keeping Track Ask children to tell how they keep track of the birthdays in their family (including their own). Show children a copy of this year's and next year's year-long calendar. Circle each of their birthdays on the calendar. Show them where they are today on the calendar. Help them each count how many days it was since their last birthday, and how many more days it will be until their next birthday.

After Sharing the Poem

Driving a Birthday Train Create a birthday train display by using markers to decorate each of twelve pieces of construction paper to resemble a train car and to label each one with the name of a different month of the year. Use a separate piece of paper to be the train engine and another to be the caboose. Display the train as a wall border. Cut "puffs of smoke" from white paper and label these with the names of the months and the children's names. Place a photo of yourself as the engineer and label the engine car with your name. As each child's birthday arrives, place a head photo of the birthday child into the car representing his or her birthday month. At month's end tally the number of birthdays celebrated that month as well as year-to-date

Home-School Connection

Family Birthday Bar Graph Provide each child with a piece of one-inch-square graph paper labeled at the bottom with the twelve months of the year. Have children interview a knowing family member to find out in which month of the year everybody else in the family celebrates his or her birthday. Children should color in the squares on the graph to show how many family birthdays occur in each month.

Telling Time with My New Dog

At seven o'clock I woke up late.
I put my clothes on inside out.
At eight o'clock I spilled my milk
and caused a mess that made me shout.

On my way to school a dog
jumped up and licked my face.
At nine o'clock that dog and I
began a speedy race.

We ran until we reached my school.
He stayed right by my side.
At ten o'clock that friendly dog
just followed me inside.

"My teacher will be mad," I thought,
"to see me late with a great big dog."
But I'd forgot—it was animal day!
The teacher had even brought a frog!

At eleven o'clock we had a show
with pets of every size.
At twelve o'clock my great new pet
and I had won a prize!

Before Sharing the Poem

Father Time's Face Have on hand a large primary instruction-type clock with hands that can be moved about freely. As you read the poem, move the hands on the clock to reflect the times mentioned. Then, let the children try moving the hands of the clock as you read.

After Sharing the Poem

Rebus Time Copy the poem onto a piece of chart pad paper, allowing for lots of space between the lines. Have children turn the poem into a rebus by drawing accurate clock faces and hands above the times mentioned in the poem. (Tip: Use a clock-face rubber stamp to press clock face images onto the chart; then, just have children add the hands to the faces so they match the times given in the poem.)

Home-School Connection

Time Out: Saturday Morning Have children keep a time log telling what they do at each hour of a Saturday morning between seven A.M. and twelve noon. If you have a clock-face rubber stamp, you can fold a piece of copy paper in quarters and stamp the clock face into each of the quadrants of the page, allowing children to write or illustrate their activities in the space remaining in each quadrant. Children may then add clock hands to the stamped-on clock faces to indicate each hour.

Telling Time on Halloween

On Halloween I told the time
With the brand new watch I wore.

I shined my flashlight on its face
While I went from door to door.

At five o'clock I saw a lion
Roaring up and down my street.

At six o'clock I saw a king
and a robot calling, "Trick or treat!"

At seven o'clock I met a monster
bigger and scarier than me.

At eight o'clock I was counting candy.
And I was a happy bumblebee.

Before Sharing the Poem

Listen and Remember Tell the class you are going to read them a poem about Halloween and that you are going to ask them some questions about the poem when you're done. After students have listened carefully, ask them to answer the following questions:

- How many different costumes were mentioned?
- Was there a pumpkin in the poem?
- Who was roaring?
- What did the child telling the poem count at the end?
- What times did the child begin and end trick-or-treating?

Have students check the poem to verify their answers.

After Sharing the Poem

Halloween Act Plan to read the poem again and select children to act out the parts. Label each child with the name of the costume he or she is supposed to be wearing. Have the child depicting the narrator show a large primary instruction-type clock and move the hands to correspond to the various times mentioned.

Home-School Connection

Watch the Watches Have children get permission to bring or wear a grown-up's watch to school for a day. Compare the features and faces on the watches. For example, have children discover how many faces are digital and how many are analog. Help children notice which watches have an hour hand, a minute hand and a second hand, and which watches need to be wound up because they work on springs, and which do not because they work on batteries. While on the subject of time, remind children to be patient with their efforts to master time. Tell them that learning time takes time!

The Baby Kangaroo

"My baby is a bright one,"
said the mother kangaroo.
"With the money in my pocket,
he knows just what to do.

He counts the nickels all by fives.
The dimes he counts by ten.
And if they drop, he quickly
picks them up and counts again.

Each time I give my son a coin
he always hollers 'thanks!'
And when he's got a lot of them,
He puts them in his bank!"

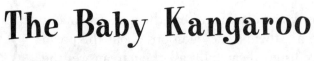

Before Sharing the Poem

What Can Money Buy? Ask children to tell if they ever get to handle real money (e.g., maybe they help the adults in their families pay for purchases; maybe they receive allowances; and maybe they actually earn, save and spend money of their own.) Ask: What would you buy if you had all the money in the world?

After Sharing the Poem

Counting Nickels In the poem, the baby kangaroo counts one hundred nickels. Provide students with ten nickels and a hundred's counting chart. Have children count the nickels by placing the first one on zero and counting up to the number 5, then continuing to count up to reach the other multiples of five:10, 15, 20, 25, 30, 35, 40, 45 and 50. Ask: How much money do you think the kangaroo would have if she had twenty nickels?

Home-School Connection

Spare Change Rubbings Have children ask to borrow the change in a family member's pocket or coin purse. The student should spread the coins out flat on a table, cover with a sheet or two of thin copy paper, and then use the side of a pencil point to create a rubbing of the coins. Have students return the coins to the owner. Then back in class, help students tally the rubbings to determine a grand total.

I Wish I Had a Nickel

I wish I had a nickel.
I wish I had a dime.
I wish I had a quarter.
I would count them all the time.

I wish I had a dollar.
But it wouldn't make a sound;
I'd never know I lost it
If it fell out on the ground.

So I'd trade it for some pennies
And I'd keep them in a sack.
I'd never ever spend them
Because then I'd want them back!

Before Sharing the Poem

Money Props Have on hand a penny, a nickel, a dime, a quarter and a dollar bill, as well as 100 pennies stored in a little bag. Use these props to demonstrate money denominations when reading the poem. Then, let children demonstrate their money sense by placing the coins down as you read. Ask: How much money do we have here in all?

After Sharing the Poem

Money Equivalencies In the poem, the poet trades the dollar bill for a sack of pennies. Ask the children to tell if they know how many pennies have to be in that sack for the trade to be fair. Show the children other money equivalencies such as two nickels for a dime, two dimes and a nickel for a quarter, four quarters for a dollar, etc. Help children understand that one coin, such as a quarter, can be worth more than several coins of lesser value, such as four pennies or four nickels. Also, point out that a dime is worth more than larger coins such as the penny or nickel. Remind children that it takes time to learn about time AND money which are both complex systems.

Home-School Connection

Money Montage Challenge children to glue down any number of coins on cardboard to create priceless works of art. Send home directions suggesting that children first experiment with placing coins into different arrangements, and then, when satisfied, gluing down the arrangement of choice. Children should also tally up the money value of their coin art before bringing back to school to display. When finished displaying, remove coins from cardboard and place back into circulation.

Notes